KLIBAN'S CATS II

D1567373

Pomegranate

SAN FRANCISCO

Pomegranate Communications, Inc.
Box 808022, Petaluma, California 94975
800-227-1428
www.pomegranate.com

Pomegranate Europe Ltd.
Unit 1, Heathcote Business Centre, Hurlbutt Road
Warwick, Warwickshire CV34 6TD, U.K.
[+44] 0 1926 430111

ISBN 0-7649-2882-1
Pomegranate Catalog No. AA245

Pomegranate publishes books of
postcards on a wide range of subjects.
Please contact the publisher for more information.

Book of postcards design by Patrice Morris
Printed in China

13 12 11 10 09 08 07 06 05 04   10 9 8 7 6 5 4 3 2 1

To facilitate detachment of the postcards from this book, fold each card along its perforation line before tearing.

A serious artist who first studied painting and design at Pratt Institute and Cooper Union, B. "Hap" Kliban (1935–1990) lived for a time in Europe, drawing incessantly and perfecting a talent for figure drawing. Returning to the United States, he worked a number of odd (!) jobs in San Francisco. One of these was a gig at the Mr. Wonderful Club, drawing the showgirls there. Between portraits of exotic dancers, Kliban drew hilarious images on cocktail napkins.

In 1962, Kliban answered an ad in *Playboy* for contributions from cartoonists, and a thirty-year relationship with that magazine was born. A cat lover, Kliban would idly sketch his four resident felines as he contemplated new ideas for *Playboy*. Those doodles found their way to a literary agent, and in 1975 Kliban's first book—called, simply, *Cat*—was published. This best-seller made the artist an overnight sensation and revolutionized animal cartooning. Although Kliban went on to publish seven other books, whose bitingly funny illustrations lampoon a range of subjects, he is best remembered for his quirky renderings of Cat and company; over a quarter-century after their debut, they still bring a smile to our faces and a warm glow to our hearts.

KLIBAN'S CATS II

Pomegranate

BOX 808022   PETALUMA   CA 94975

KLIBAN'S CATS II

Pomegranate

BOX 808022   PETALUMA   CA 94975

KLIBAN'S CATS II

Pomegranate

BOX 808022   PETALUMA   CA 94975

KLIBAN'S CATS II

Pomegranate

BOX 808022   PETALUMA   CA 94975

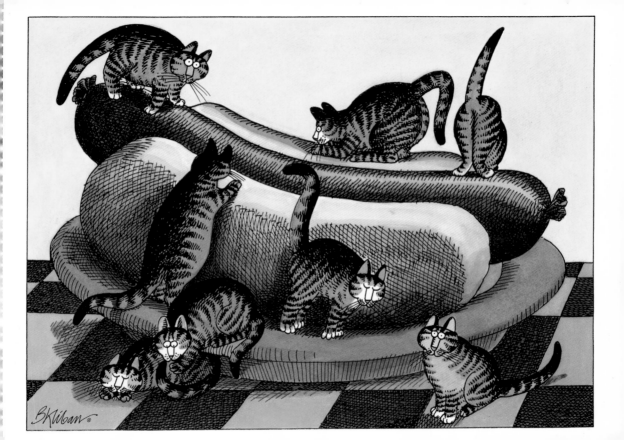

KLIBAN'S CATS II

Pomegranate

BOX 808022   PETALUMA   CA 94975

KLIBAN'S CATS II

Pomegranate

BOX 808022   PETALUMA   CA 94975

KLIBAN'S CATS II

Pomegranate

BOX 808022   PETALUMA   CA 94975

KLIBAN'S CATS II

Pomegranate

BOX 808022   PETALUMA   CA 94975

KLIBAN'S CATS II

BOX 808022   PETALUMA   CA 94975

Pomegranate

KLIBAN'S CATS II

BOX 808022   PETALUMA   CA 94975

Pomegranate

KLIBAN'S CATS II

Pomegranate

BOX 808022 PETALUMA CA 94975

KLIBAN'S CATS II

Pomegranate

BOX 808022　PETALUMA　CA 94975

KLIBAN'S CATS II

BOX 808022   PETALUMA   CA 94975

Pomegranate

KLIBAN'S CATS II

Pomegranate

BOX 808022   PETALUMA   CA 94975

KLIBAN'S CATS II

BOX 808022   PETALUMA   CA 94975

Pomegranate

KLIBAN'S CATS II

Pomegranate

BOX 808022   PETALUMA   CA 94975

KLIBAN'S CATS II

Pomegranate

BOX 808022   PETALUMA   CA 94975

KLIBAN'S CATS II

BOX 808022   PETALUMA   CA 94975

Pomegranate

KLIBAN'S CATS II

Pomegranate

BOX 808022   PETALUMA   CA 94975

KLIBAN'S CATS II

Pomegranate

BOX 808022   PETALUMA   CA 94975

KLIBAN'S CATS II

Pomegranate

BOX 808022　PETALUMA　CA 94975

KLIBAN'S CATS II

Pomegranate

BOX 808022 PETALUMA CA 94975

KLIBAN'S CATS II

Pomegranate

BOX 808022   PETALUMA   CA 94975

KLIBAN'S CATS II

Pomegranate

BOX 808022　PETALUMA　CA 94975

KLIBAN'S CATS II

BOX 808022   PETALUMA   CA 94975

Pomegranate

KLIBAN'S CATS II

BOX 808022 PETALUMA CA 94975

Pomegranate

KLIBAN'S CATS II

Pomegranate

BOX 808022   PETALUMA   CA 94975

KLIBAN'S CATS II

Pomegranate

BOX 808022   PETALUMA   CA 94975

KLIBAN'S CATS II

Pomegranate

BOX 808022   PETALUMA   CA 94975

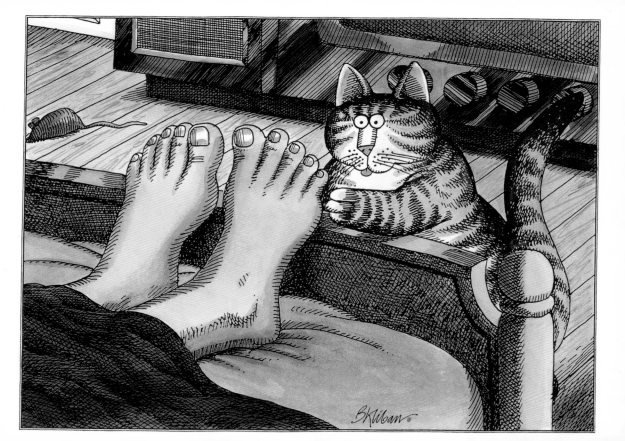

KLIBAN'S CATS II

Pomegranate

BOX 808022 PETALUMA CA 94975